My Cross

ALL IRAQIS Are Going To

H E L L!

"George W. Bush"
and
"The Christian Right"

by

Reno Jean Daret, III, B.S., M.Ed.

Copyright © 2005 by Reno Jean Daret, III

All rights reserved. No part of this book may be reproduced or transmitted in any form or by any means, electronic or mechanical, including photocopy, recording or any information storage or retrieval system, without prior permission in writing from the author.

ISBN: 0-9661812-7-1

Library of Congress Catalog Number
Pending

Published by Lycanthrope Press
P.O. Box 9028
Metairie, LA 70005-9028
(504) 866-9756 - office
(504) 866-7161 - FAX

Dedication

*This book is dedicated to
my mother and father to whom
I owe everything.
Mom and Dad, I love you forever.*

"The mind is its own place, and in itself, can make heaven of Hell, and a hell of Heaven" (John Milton).

"This is my simple religion. There is no need for temples; no need for complicated philosophy. Our own brain, our own heart is our temple; the philosophy is kindness" (The Dalai Lama).

"The world is my country, all mankind are my brethren, and to do good is my religion" (Thomas Paine).

CONTENTS

CHAPTER I 3
    George W. Bush
    The Secret Plot to Conquer the World

CHAPTER II 19
    An Invitation
    The Meaning of Life

CHAPTER III 23
    Question #1
    Is Christianity an exclusive religion?

CHAPTER IV 37
    Question #2
    Do we learn about God by reading the Bible?

CHAPTER V 43
    Question #3
    How does this world we live in work?

CHAPTER VI 51
    Question #4
    Do You Eat Your God?

CHAPTER VII 55
    Question #5
    Is Mary "Ever Virgin?"
    Did Jesus have brothers?

CHAPTER VIII 59
  Question #6
  What is the Christian view?

CHAPTER IX 61
  The Supernatural
  Question #7
  Do you believe in a whole host of supernatural beings?

CHAPTER X 63
  Question #8
  Does God do miracles?

CHAPTER XI 65
  Question #9
  Were they Greek or Christian ideas?

CHAPTER XII 69
  Question #10
  Can we know about Jesus by reading the Bible?

CHAPTER XIII 75
  Question #11
  Did good Christians profess hatred for the Jews?

CHAPTER XIV 79
  Question #12
  The Cross

CHAPTER XV 83
    Question #13
    Mithraism

CHAPTER XVI 93
    Question #14
    Are you Normal?

CHAPTER XVII 97
    Did You Know?

CHAPTER XVIII 101
    What Do You Believe?

CHAPTER XIX 105
    The Maltese Cross

ANNOTATED BIBLIOGRAPHY 107

BELIEVING 111

BOOK ORDERING INFORMATION 112

INTRODUCTION

Here is a quote from the *Passover Plot* by Hugh Schonfield. I place it here because it expresses my feelings precisely.

> I fully realize that my treatment of the subject may cause considerable debate and controversy. I cannot undertake to answer all comments whether in personal letters or in the Press; but I will welcome them, and if this is warranted I will do my best to reply in a further book. Where I have had to challenge traditional beliefs it has not been with any hostile intent, and I hope therefore that criticism will be temperate and confined to persuasion on the basis of evidence. If I have had an objective, other than patient seeking after truth, it has been to be of helpful service in providing people today with a more correct understanding of Christ, which they can live with and from which they can draw courage and inspiration, especially those in adversity and despondency. If it can be shown that to follow Jesus means to imbibe his spirit and seek his ends for mankind then these pages may have made a timely and constructive contribution to one of the most vital dialogues of this generation.[1]

---

[1] The Passover Plot, Hugh J. Schonfield

I, unlike Hugh Schonfield, do not have to say I cannot undertake to answer all comments; because, now in 2005, thanks to the Internet, everyone can see everyone else's comments on this book and can share their own comments with the entire world. Please join us in this discussion and seeking of truth and peace and God at WWW.LIVEJOURNAL.COM then search DEEPTRUTHINFO or come to the web site WWW.DEEPTRUTH.INFO

God Be With You,

Reno Jean Daret, III

CHAPTER I

George W. Bush is a Christian man. He is a member of Highland Park United Methodist Church. George W. Bush is a very religious man and he believes in Jesus and the Bible.

George W. Bush saved the people of the world from the cruel dictator tyrant Saddam Hussein. Bush believes he is doing God's good work by defeating and ending evil. He uses biblical language when he speaks. He sees the world through his deeply religious Christian prospective. He calls himself a "Born-Again Christian."

George W. Bush believes he was elected president as part of God's divine plan. He believes now is the time for God's kingdom to come and God's will to be done on earth. George W. Bush believes he is on a mission from God to Christianize the whole world. George W. Bush believes like all Christians:

John 3:16
> For God so loved the world, that he gave his only begotten Son, that whosoever believeth in him should not perish but have everlasting life.

John 14:6
> Jesus said "I am the way and the truth and the life. No one comes to the Father except through me."

John 3:18
> He that believeth in him is not condemned, but he that believeth not is condemned already, because he has not believed in the name of the only Son of God.

These bible verses say that to be saved to have everlasting life in heaven with God, you must believe in Jesus as the Son of God. Everlasting life is life that lasts for billions and billions of years and even longer than that–to be in paradise with God and Jesus forever for eternity.

But for those who do not have everlasting life their fate is to go to hell. Their life is just this brief physical life on earth with a life expectancy of 50-80 years, then eternity in hell.

What a difference in your concept of who a person is when you believe that person will have eternal life. How much different is your concept of who a person is when you believe that person will only live for a brief second compared to eternity. How insignificant that "brief second" person becomes compared to you when you know you will live forever. Christians will live forever with God but non-Christians will die and go to hell; this is what Christianity teaches and this is what George W. Bush believes.

Christianity is an exclusive religion that teaches that only Christians will be with God and have eternal life.

All Iraqis are going to hell–that is what George W. Bush and the Christian Right believe. The goal of Born-Again and Evangelical Christians is to Christianize the whole world. When Lt. Gen. William G. Boykin says, "The war against militant Islam is a battle against Satan" and then goes on to say "Muslims worship an idol and not a real God" he is expressing the view of all Christian believers in Jesus. Now, Boykin has been muzzled by George W. Bush because the deep truth cannot be told to the masses of people in the world.

If you are Christian like George W. Bush, you believe all other religions are false religions and it is your duty to convert them to Christianity so they will know Jesus and have everlasting life. So if Muslims do not denounce the religion of their forefathers and convert to Christianity, they will go to hell.

Christian leaders have said publicly that "God put George Bush in the White House." "It is the will of God that George Bush is President," so he can do God's good work. These religious leaders and George W. Bush believe that spreading the "Good News" of Jesus throughout the world is their mission and George W. Bush wants the big banner to read **"Mission Accomplished."**

George Bush is interested in souls. He called his election campaign tour the "Heart and Soul" of America Tour. When he met with Russian leader Valdimir Putin, Bush said, "I got a sense of his soul."

Senator Richard Bird has publicly warned that George W. Bush is the most dangerous president in the last 100 years. He leads with his gut instinct, but he is a *born-again Christian*–now, how dangerous can that be?

All Iraqis are going to hell–that is what George W. Bush and the Christian Right believe. The relationship of Christians with non-Christians throughout history is a horror story. Christians dealing with non-Christians has been horrific for the Incas, Aztecs, Mayans, Native North Americans, Black Slaves, Jews and members of any non-Christian religion.

Only Christians, believers in Christ, are saved when Jesus comes back to earth. When the rapture occurs, all non-believers, Jews, Hindus, Buddhists, Muslims–all will be cast into hell and death and pain, but all true believers in Jesus will be raised up to heaven to be with God forever.

So, if some Muslims are killed by accident as collateral damage when the military goes after terrorist criminals who deserve to be killed, does it really matter? They are not Christian people anyway. They are only Indians, Jews, Negroes, Hindus, Buddhists, Muslims.

Even before the war started we basically had Saddam Hussein neutralized with *two no-fly zones* and inspectors on the ground in Iraq plus satellites and drone spy planes. Saddam could not make a move without our knowing it.

If George Bush went to war to neutralize the threat to the world from Saddam Hussein, he could have accomplished the same objective by sending 100,000 inspectors instead of 140,000 U.S. troops. It would have been a lot cheaper financially and over 20,000 people would not now be dead. Saddam was allowing inspectors but George Bush pulled them out because they could not find *weapons of mass destruction* (WMD).

Saddam said he had no WMD; he even invited the CIA to come to Iraq and show the inspectors where the weapons of mass destruction were. But George W. Bush pulled the inspectors and attacked. He really did not want to neutralize Saddam Hussein, he wanted to put Saddam out of power. He wants to punish Saddam. Now George W. Bush can do God's work in Iraq and maybe the whole world.

What happened at Abu Ghraib Prison was a seminal moment in the war. How could those Christians do those things to those Muslims? The abuses did not just happen at Abu Ghraib, it happened throughout the American-controlled prisons in Iraq and Afghanistan. Go to Google on the Internet and see for yourself. See what was done!

If you type in "Abu Ghraib," Google gives you 139,000 web site listings; if you type in "Iraq Prison Abuse," you get 208,000 web site listings and if you type in "Photos of Iraqi Prisoner Abuse," you get 145,000 web site listings to go to. This abuse has spawned hatred that will take generations to abate. These photos will never be forgotten. This is an absolute tragedy and absolute disaster. But don't be too shocked, read this:

The Wrath of
The Inquisition:
Torture, Terror or Death

France: To obtain confessions the Inquisition in Toulouse built a roaring fire and grilled their victims' feet. Fat or grease was rubbed on the feet to insure maximum agony.

Italy: Two hundred heretics were burned in an arena. The spectacle drew a large crowd that February day in 1278. The bones of a man who had been dead for sixty-three years were exhumed and also burned, and his estate was confiscated, because he had been condemned by the Inquisition.

Spain: Victims were frequently roasted in their own blood, over a slow fire, so they would suffer the maximum pain. In the latter half of the seventeenth century, the steel torture chair was designed to wring shrieking agony from every nerve in the victim's body. It was fitted with manacles for the feet and hands, a helmet studded with screws to pierce the ear drums, rupture the nose and crush the chin, a gag with rack action that drew the tongue forward until it tore loose from the mouth, and thumb screws and screw-forceps for ripping out finger and toe nails.

The Netherlands: A man sentenced to be burned alive would often be prevented from talking by having his tongue screwed tightly between two irons. The tongue would then be branded with a hot iron so that it would swell and could not be drawn back into the mouth.[2]

I challenge George W. Bush, William Boykin, Ralph Reed, Billy Graham, David Limbaugh, Jimmy Swaggart, Pat Robertson, Roy Moore, Jerry Falwell, Charles Stanley, Benny Hinn, Leroy Jenkins, Jimmy Swaggart, Franklin Graham (who called the religion of Islam "Wicked and Violent), Anne Graham Lotz, James Robison, Arthur Blessitt, and Dr. Ted Haggard (President of the National Association of Evangelicals) to say they believe Muslim, Iraqis will be saved and be with God and have everlasting life without converting to Christianity without believing Jesus Christ is the Son of God. They will not say Muslims are going to heaven because they will not deny Christ and the teaching of their exclusive religion that the only people going to heaven and having everlasting life are Christians. They confirm their beliefs every Sunday when they attend church. So they try to convert everyone to the "true religion"–Christianity.

George W. Bush believes the war has been worth the cost. Now the Iraqis are saved from the evil Saddam Hussein. George W. Bush believes over 20,000 deaths and 100,000 injuries and pain and suffering and four hundred billion ($400,000,000,000) dollars spent is the price he is willing to pay for V I C T O R Y!

He has freed the Iraqis people from fear, pain and death at the hands of Saddam Hussein.

If George W. Bush did this to save the people of Iraq from Saddam Hussein, what would he do to save the people of Iraq from the Devil and Hell?

George W. Bush believes unless Iraqis convert to Christianity, they will go to a place where every one of

---

[2]The Inquisition: Macmillan Publishing Co., Inc., No. 59140.

them will experience fear, pain and death at the hands of Satan. But it will not be the short 35 years that Saddam ruled them, it will be eternity that the Devil himself will rule them.

Why did George Bush invade Iraq? He invaded to make Iraq a free democratic society. Then Christians with all their money and influence, movies and TV, and rock-and-roll and blue jeans and WalMart and McDonalds can convert the Iraqis and the rest of the Middle East to Christianity. George Bush wants to do something big. He is a *born-again Christian* and wants to convert the whole world to Jesus and Christianity. So, the 20,000 Iraqis that have died so far in the war went to hell. Kill'em or convert them is what some say is happening. Millions of dollars are spent every day by Christian organizations and missionaries in an effort to win souls to Christ.

To stamp out other religions is the desired effect. George Bush is a *born-again Christian*. How dangerous can that be? This Iraqi war is a war between good and evil, between Christians and non-Christians. The ultimate goal is to Christianize the whole world–then there will be peace.

What Others Are Saying About George W. Bush and His Presidency

1. "To this aggressive extension of American power in the world, President George W. Bush adds God–and that changes the picture dramatically.

    "It's one thing for a nation to assert its raw dominance in the world; it's quite another to suggest . . . that his presidency may be a divine appointment for a time such as this" (Jim Wallis, "Sojourner Magazine)[3].

2. "One thing I've learned in my life is never to trust anyone who thinks that he exclusively has God on his side, especially when he's the president of the U.S." (Richard Gere, Actor/Political Activist).[4]

3. "Of course as a self-described 'messenger' of God who was praying for strength to do the Lord's will, 'Bush was not troubled about shedding a little secular document called the U.S. Constitution'" (Robert Sheer, "LA Times).[5]

4. "Talk about separation of church and state; it's not separate at all in Bush's brain. He's an unsuitable office holder" (Ralph Nader, President Hopeful, Consumer Crusader).[6]

5. " . . . this presidency–is the most resolutely, 'faith-based' in modern times, an enterprise founded, supported and guided by trust in the temporal and spiritual power of God" (Howard Fineman. 2003. "Newsweek Magazine").[7]

---

[3]Wallis, Jim. "Sojourner Magazine."

[4]Gere, Richard. Actor/Political Activist.

[5]Sheer, Robert. "LA Times."

[6]Nader, Ralph, President Hopeful, Consumer Crusader.

[7]Fineman, H. 2003. "Newsweek."

6. "Nobody spends more time on his knees than George W. Bush. The Bush administration hums to the sound of prayer. Prayer meetings take place day and night. It's not uncommon to see White House functionaries hurrying down corridors carrying Bibles" (Justin Webb, British Broadcasting Company Correspondent)[8].

7. "Bush's 'National Security Strategy' amounts to an enormously presumptuous agenda for domination of the entire world . . . " (Robert Higgs, Alternet)[9]

THE SECRET PLOT TO CONQUER THE WORLD

TIME: The meetings and planning went on for a week in April 1984.

THE PLACE: Hotel Room Holiday Inn, Midland, Texas

THE PLOTTERS: Arthur Blessitt
Jim Sales
George W. Bush

Arthur Blessitt: World Evangelist, The Man Who Carried the Cross Around the World in Every Nation. The World's Longest Walk as listed in the Guinness Book of Records. Now 303 Nations, 36,651 miles and still Walking! Started Christmas 1969!

---

[8]Webb, Justin. British Broadcasting Company Correspondent.

[9]Higgs, Robert. Alternet

Jim Sales, Texas Oilman, who arranged the meeting.

George W. Bush, son of Vice President George H. Bush. George W. Bush worked in the Bush/Reagan campaign for president in 1984. Ronald Reagan was president from 1980 to 1988 and used the awesome power of the presidency to set in motion forces that would bring down the Berlin Wall.

The Plot: Influence or control the presidency of the United States and use that awesome power to spread the cross and Jesus Christ over every nation. They joined hands and prayed that the mission of bringing the gospel of Jesus Christ and the cross and Christianity to every nation would be successful. They prayed "Thy kingdom come, God's will be done, on earth as it is in heaven," and for George W. Bush God's kingdom and God's will is that "Jesus be adored by every land and nation. Jesus is the salvation of the world."

George W. Bush believes when he was out running three miles in Colorado Springs in July 1986 that he had an encounter with God. "My faith is an integral part of my whole being, that's what faith is, I don't think you can separate your faith from who you are" (George W. Bush, "Maranatha Christian Journal, 2000).[10]

The evangelist Billy Graham spent several days in intense conversations and meeting with George W. Bush in 1985. These meetings took place at the Bush family

---

[10]Bush, George W. 2000, October 12. "Maranatha Christian Journal."

compound in Kennebunkport, Maine. George W. Bush has publicly expressed his vision to spread democracy over the entire world. Spreading democracy over the entire world is part of his even grander plan to spread Christianity to all 303 nations of the earth.

Now, we see in Iraq the plan being implemented to conquer the world, democratize Iraq, spend billions to make it an economic success and send evangelists to Christianize Iraq. Other nations will see a wonderful Iraq and democracy and Christianity will spread over the Middle East and then the entire world. This is the plan to spread democracy and Christianity over the entire world.

Can George W. Bush bring the cross to every nation like Arthur Blessitt has physically done? So dear reader, do you think George W. Bush and Arthur Blessitt would want to put the cross over Muslim, Buddhist, and Hindu nations? "Go into all the world and preach the gospel to every person" (Mark 16:15).

> Prayer and reading our Bible daily is to strengthen us and help enable us to bear witness of Jesus to others. We should seek to witness for Jesus to every person we meet wherever we are we should not be fearful or timid, but we should be loving and open as we tell others of Jesus, we are saved to share our faith not simply to wait until Jesus comes to receive us. Our commission is to go into the entire world and preach the gospel to every person (http://www.blessitt.com/bush.html)[11]

How could they dare to do this unless they believe in their hearts and souls that they are doing God's good work? George W. Bush and Arthur Blessitt believe that

---

[11]http://www.blessitt.com/bush.html

they are part of a divine plan to Christianize the entire world. Does what I am writing here sound untrue and outrageous? Does it sound preposterous to you that anyone would actually think it is right to impose the cross on others? Read on, because one of the plotters is ready to contribute to the plan.

"News Flash, launch date set for January 26, 2005! Glory

The cross will be over You personally! The Cross will be over every Nation on earth! Over Afghanistan! Saudi Arabia! Jerusalem! America! The cross in Space Satellite will be in a Polar orbit from pole to pole. As the earth turns it will pass over every inch of the earth like peeling an apple. The cross will circle the earth every one and a half hours. After launch we can tell you on our site when it will be over you and your nation. We have carried the cross in Every nation. Now we will, God willing have it flying above Every nation! We wave the cross in the face of Satan and proclaim that Jesus is Lord over All the Earth. All glory to God.

Historic launch of the First Cross in Orbit Around the Earth!"[12]

"Then the Sign of the Son of Man will appear in the Sky! Then all the tribes of the earth will mourn and they will see the Son of Man coming on the clouds of heaven with power and great glory" (Matthew 24:30).

---

[12]http://www.blessitt.com/crossinspace/index.html

"Come after me and I will make you fishers of men" (Matthew 4:19).

The Christians are the fishermen and the non-Christians are the fish. The non-Christians must be caught on the hook of Christianity.

"We wave the cross in the face of <u>Satan</u> and proclaim that Jesus is Lord over all the earth"
"Over Afghanistan! Saudi Arabia! Jerusalem!"[13]
George W. Bush is a **Born-Again Christian**. Now how dangerous can that be?

"Onward, Christian soldiers, marching as to war,
With the cross of Jesus going on before,
Christ, the royal Master, leads against the foe;
Forward into battle see His banners go!

Refrain

What the saints established that I hold true,
What the saints believed, that I believe too.
Long as earth endureth, men the faith will hold,
Kingdoms, nations, empires, in destruction rolled.

Refrain

Crowns and thrones may perish, kingdoms rise and
 wane,
But the church of Jesus constant will remain.
Gates of hell can never gainst that church prevail;

---

[13]http://www.blessitt.com/crossinspace/index.html

We have Christ's own promise, and that cannot fail."[14]

"Onward Christian soldiers. Conservative fundamentalists with close ties to President Bush are planning a anew missionary push in Iraq – and they might already be converting U.S. troops to their cause.

Among them Charles Stanley, the former two-time president of the Southern Baptist Convention and close ally of former President George Bush and a fervent supporter of the current president's war on Iraq.

'The government is ordained by God with the right to promote good and restrain evil,' Stanley said in his sermon. 'This includes wickedness that exists within the nation, as well as any wicked persons or countries that threaten foreign nations. Therefore, a government has biblical grounds to go to war in the nation's defense or to liberate others in the world who are enslaved.'

Through Stanley's bellicose sermon targets an American audience, it was almost certainly heard across the Arab world, as his sermons are translated into Arabic by In Touch and beamed from Benghazi, Libya, to Tehran, Iran, each week by satellite TV and radio. But while Saddam maintained his iron grip, In Touch could broadcast to Iraq only by shortwave radio; now that the regime has fallen, the ministry could be presented with a bevy of opportunities. The

---

[14]Baring-Gould, Sabine. (1865).

opportunity for broadcast expansion in postwar Iraq is 'phenomenal.'

Already, churches and ministries on the religious right are poised to send in missionaries and to amp up broadcast to the region. Like advanced troops before the invasion, some U.S. military officials in Iraq have already staked out the country as a natural place to spread the Christian Gospel."[15]

"Go, therefore, and make disciples of all nations, baptizing them in the name of the Father, and of the Son, and of the Holy spirit, teaching them to observe all that I have commanded you" (Matthew, 28:19-20).

"I do not believe in the creed professed by the Jewish Church, by the Roman Church, by the Greek Church, by the Turkish Church, by the Protestant Church, nor by any church that I know of. My own mind is my own church" (Paine, Thomas).

"Everybody likes to go their own way–to choose their own time and manner of devotion."[16]

"It is a fine thing to establish one's own religion in one's heart, not to be dependent on tradition and

---

[15] Blumenthal, M. (2003). Retrieved from Salon.com News - Onward Christian soldiers.

[16] Austen, Jane. (1775-1817). Mansfield Park.

second-hand ideals. Life will seem to you, later, not a lesser, but a greater thing."[17]

"Everyone ought to worship God according to his own inclinations, and not to be constrained by force."[18]

"If a man does not keep pace with his companions, perhaps it is because he hears a different drummer. Let him step to the music he hears, however measured or far away."[19]

"I want you to just let a wave of intolerance wash over you. I want you to let a wave of hatred wash over you. Yes, hate is good . . . Our goal is a Christian nation. We have a Biblical duty, we are called by God, to conquer this country. We don't want equal time. We don't want pluralism." (Terry Randall)[20]

"I want to be invisible. I do guerrilla warfare. I paint my face and travel at night. You don't know it's over until you're in a body bag." (Ralph Reed)[21]

---

[17]Lawrence, D. H.

[18]Josephus, Flavius. (37 c.e. - 100 c.e.) *Life.*

[19]Thoreau, Henry David.

[20]Terry, Randall, Founder of Operation Rescue. *The News-Sentinel.* Fort Wayne, Indiana, 8-16-93.

[21]Reed, Ralph. Norfolk Virginian-Pilot, 11/9/91.

CHAPTER II

An Invitation

Dear Reader,

We, as members of the same species, "Homo Sapiens," have certain characteristics in common. We have similar emotions, needs, desires, fears and thought patterns. In the last 40 years we have come to know the actions and experiences of more members of our species than was ever before possible.

Our species lives 20 years longer; the older members have the wisdom of long life. Yet, the questions that have haunted men's minds since the dawn of history seem even more complicated.

Some of these questions along with other related questions are contained in this book *All Iraqis Are Going to Hell: "George W. Bush" and "The Christian Right"* by staring the questions in the eye and giving a precise answer, we move closer to the truth, and moving closer to the truth is moving closer to God.

Verbal answers are lost in the wind and can lead to heated discussion. Written answers are done with much thought and are messages for the next generation. So, dear reader, do you dare spend time pondering the meaning of life? Do you dare to ask, "What's it all about?" "How does this place work?" And, give your unflinching answer to homo sapiens who follow you in this experience of life on earth.

Reference material follows the fourteen questions. The information contained therein was usually the stimulus for the question being formed. The majority of books used as reference information are taken from the *Bible*. In one sense this is real *Bible* study. Study the reference material, study other materials, study the *Bible*. Give thoughtful and truthful answers. Let's talk religion!

Come to the web site deeptruth.info or <u>www.livejournal.com then search www.deepthruthinfo</u> Come express your thoughts. Let's seek the truth together. Let's seek harmony and peace and happiness for all the people of the world through love and truth. Let's seek God together.

Go to the web site <u>www.deeptruth.info</u> and click on the your comments link and post your uncensored comments for the world to read.

You can also go to <u>www.livejournal.com</u>; open a free account; then as a member you can use the search feature to go to <u>deeptruthinfo</u>. When you click <u>deeptruthinfo</u> it will take you to the "God Is Love" Community On Line Journal. Click on the pencil icon and place your uncensored comments for the whole world to read.

The Meaning of Life

What is the meaning of life?

The purpose of life is to make life meaningful by doing something of merit for your fellow man; to make the world a better, happier, more peaceful place for all of humankind to be as one with the Divine Absolute.

Again, I invite you to go to www.deeptruth.info or www.livejournal.com then search deeptruthinfo and tell the world your views on the meaning of life.

Your life has validity and the world is a better place when you spread love. Love one another; this is the message.

When we act in a loving way toward other people we are manifesting God. God is inside every person and in every religion. God is love.

"When I do good, I feel good; when I do bad, I feel bad, and that is my religion."[22]

"Imagine all the people living life in Peace . . .
You may say I'm a dreamer, but I'm not the only one . . .
I hope some day you join us, and the world will live as one."[23]

---

[22]Lincoln, Abraham. (1809-1865).

[23]Lennon, John

CHAPTER III

Question #1

Is Christianity an exclusive religion? Does Christianity say that anyone who **does** not believe Jesus Christ is the Son of God is condemned and **will not** be with God and **will** perish and **will not** have everlasting life? What does the Christian *Bible* say?

John 3:18
He that believeth in him is not condemned but he that believeth not is condemned already, because he hath not believed in the . . . only begotten Son of God.

John 14:6
Jesus said, "I am the way and the truth and the life; no one comes to the father but by me."

John 3:16
For God so loved the world, that he gave his only begotten Son, that whosoever believeth in Him should not perish, but have everlasting life.

John 5:12
He who has the Son has life; he who does not have the Son of God does not have life.

John 5:13
   I write these things to you who believe in the name of the Son of God so that you may know that you have eternal life.

John 1:12
   Believe that Jesus Christ died for your sins and ask him to be your savior. "As many as received Him, to them he gave power to become the Sons of God, even to them that believe in his name."

Romans 10:9
   Confess the Lord Jesus Christ before men. "If thou shalt confess with thy mouth the Lord Jesus, and shalt believe in thine heart that God hath raised Him from the dead, thou shalt be saved."

Timothy 2:5
   For there is one God, and one mediator between God and men, the man Christ Jesus.

Acts 16:31
   They replied, "Believe in the Lord Jesus, and you will be saved–you and your household."

Acts 4:10
   Then know this, you and all the people of Israel: It is by the name of Jesus Christ of Nazareth, whom you crucified but whom God raised from the dead, that this man stands before you healed.

Acts 4:12
   Salvation is found in no one else, for there is no other name under heaven given to men by which we must be saved.

I John 5:11
    And this is the testimony: God has given us eternal life, and this life is in his Son.

I John 2:23
    No one who denies the Son has the Father; whoever acknowledges the Son has the Father also.

John 5:23
    That all may honor the Son just as they honor the Father. He who does not honor the Son does not honor the Father who sent him.

Luke 10:22
    "All things have been committed to me by my Father. No one knows who the Son is except the Father, and no one knows who the Father is except the Son and those to whom the Son chooses to reveal Him."

Luke 13:3
    I tell you, No! But unless you repent, you too will all perish.

John 3:36
    "He that believeth in the Son hath everlasting life: and he that believeth not the Son shall not see life."

2 Thessalonians 1:8, 9
    ". . . when 'with flaming power he will inflict punishment on those who do not acknowledge God nor heed' the good news of our Lord Jesus. Such as these will suffer the penalty of eternal ruin apart from the presence of the Lord and the glory of his might."

Romans 6:23
"For the wages of sin is death; but the gift of God is eternal life through Jesus Christ our Lord."

Revelations 20:15
". . . anyone whose name was not found inscribed in the book of the living was hurled into this pool of fire."

Question #1

The message of these 19 *Bible* verses is that only believers in Jesus Christ will be saved and have everlasting life. The rest of the message is that non-believers will not be with God and will not have everlasting life.

Do Christians actually believe that only they will be in heaven with God and the non-believers the non-Christians in the world (66% of the people in the world Buddhist, Hindus, Muslims, Jews, and other godfearing people) are going to hell?

4,000,000,000 people (four billion people). How could God let this happen? But wait, there is hope for all these lost souls, for Christians practice evangelism. They will send missionaries to spread the good news of Jesus and convert the lost souls. They will witness for Christ and bring souls to Christianity.

Here is a challenge to every Christian. Write a one page letter to the children of all the other non-Christian religions of the world. In the letter to Muslims, Hindus, Buddhists, and Jews—what would you tell them?

Would you say that they should follow the religion of their parents or should they change (convert) to your religion? Would you tell them that they should convert to your true religion to be with Jesus and God and have eternal salvation or would you tell them to follow the religion of their parents? Tell them where their souls will be if they are non-Christian when they die. Tell them exactly what they must do to have everlasting life. Tell them what actions you believe they must take.

Here is the space for your one-page letter. I challenge you to write it!

Letter to Non-Christian Children of the World

Dear Children,

Christian teaching says that millions and millions of good moral God-seeking people will not have everlasting life and be with God because they are not believing in the true religion–Christianity.

The "How to Respond Series" is a series of ten topics written for Christians so they will have the knowledge and insight to defend their faith as well as to witness confidently to Jesus Christ. In *How to Respond to Islam* by Philip H. Lochhaas, he stated "

How to Respond to Islam urges Christians to show respect toward Muslims, but it also emphasizes that no person can have eternal salvation apart from the grace of God in Jesus Christ alone.[24]

Here is a quote from another book, *Christianity and Islam Are Missionary Faiths*.
. . . Christians should have respect toward Muslims as persons and seekers after God, but it also emphasizes that no person, no matter how devout and respectable he may be, can possess truth and eternal salvation apart from the grace of God in Jesus Christ alone. The one *vital* difference between Christianity and Islam is not political or economic. It is spiritual. "What do you think of the Christ? Whose son is He?" (Matt. 22:42). Upon the answer to that question hangs the eternal destiny of every person. Jesus said: "I am the Way, and the Truth, and the Life; no one comes to the Father but by me" (John 14:6).

---

[24]Lochhaas, Philip H. *How to Respond to Islam*. St. Louis: Concordia Publishing House.

There can be no compromise or surrender of that eternal Word.[25]

The eternal destiny of Iraqi Muslims is hell because they are not Christian. Here is a copy of a Christian pamphlet by William MacDonald.

Am I Going to Heaven?
Instructions

A Check below what you feel is the best basis for reaching Heaven.

- ☐ 1. Keeping the Ten Commandments.
- ☐ 2. Gifts to charity.
- ☐ 3. Doing one's best.
- ☐ 4. Leading a good life.
- ☐ 5. Good works.
- ☐ 6. Trying to obey the Golden Rule.
- ☐ 7. Tithing or giving to the church.
- ☐ 8. Church membership.
- ☐ 9. Regular church attendance.
- ☐ 10. Prayers.
- ☐ 11. Fasting.
- ☐ 12. Baptism
- ☐ 13. Holy Communion.
- ☐ 14. Born of Christian parents.
- ☐ 15. Confirmation.
- ☐ 16. Penances.
- ☐ 17. Extreme unction.

---

[25]Ibid, p. 10.

B Now proceed to the next page and find out if, according to God's Word, you're on the way to Heaven.

Explanation

1. Though the Ten Commandments are God's absolute standards of conduct, no mortal has ever fully kept His laws, nor could one reach Heaven by trying. The Bible states:
   > Therefore by the deeds of the law there shall no flesh be justified in His (God's) sight: for by the law is the knowledge of sin (Romans 3:20).

2, 3, or 4. These are commendable acts, but according to God's Word, they will never save anyone:
   > Not by works of righteousness which we have done, but according to His mercy He saved us (Titus 3:5).

5, 6, or 7. God's clear declaration is:
   > For by grace are ye saved through faith; and that not of yourselves: it is the gift of God: not of works, lest any man should boast (Ephesians 2:8, 9).

8, 9, 10 or 11. Although these things are good in themselves, they can never justify sinners before a holy God:
   > We are all as an unclean thing, and all our righteousnesses are as filthy rags (Isaiah 64:6).

12 or 13. Without trusting in Jesus Christ, Baptism and

Communion cannot help. The Bible shows clearly that these are of spiritual value only when one believes in Jesus Christ.
(See Acts 8:12, 1 Corinthians 11:2, 23-32)

14. Children born into Christian homes need to be saved like anyone else.

As many as received Him [Christ], to them gave He power to become the sons of God, even to them that believe on His Name; which were born, not of blood [not of one's parentage], nor of the will of the flesh, nor of the will of man, but of God (John 1:12, 13).

15, 16, 17. As the basis for going to Heaven, none of these is the real issue. A person could well go through all of these actions without having settled the real issue of salvation.

What then is God's way of salvation? The Bible gives a definite answer. The one and only means of spending eternity with God in Heaven is *faith* in the Lord Jesus Christ alone. Because we cannot save ourselves by good works, good character, personal effort, or merit of any kind, God sent His Son to die as a substitute for sinners. When the Lord Jesus died on Calvary and rose again the third day, He finished the work necessary for salvation. Now all that God requires is that we receive Christ as our Savior: "Believe in the Lord Jesus Christ, and thou salt be saved" (Acts 16:31).
Thus when the sinner trusts the Savior, he is saved, and on the authority of God's Word has everlasting life and is bound for Heaven.

Jesus said, "He that heareth My word, and believeth in Him that sent Me, hath everlasting life, and shall not come into condemnation; but is passed from death unto life" (John 5:24).

Will you accept God's way of salvation? The choice is yours. You may continue to trust in those things listed on page 21. If so, you will go to the grave without Christ, and wake up in a lost eternity. Or you may believe in Jesus and be saved.

Be wise! Choose Christ! Then indicate the choice you have made below.

"My hopes for Heaven are based completely upon the Lord Jesus Christ, my Lord and my savior."[26]

So Christians pray that non-Christians will convert. Should they use economic persuasion, force, or even torture to accomplish their mission?

Christians have many different little books called Tracks. They give them out to spread world Christianity. Here is one sample page taken from just one of these many different "Tracks."

---

[26]MacDonald, William, "Am I Going to Heaven?"

One of Satan's Greatest Weapons is Religion . . . Here Are Only a Few of His Religions and Gimmicks:			
• Scientology	• Maoism	• Hari Krishna	• E.S.P.
• Bahat	• Judahism	• Jehovah Witnesses	• Ouija Boards
• Theosophy	• Church of Satan	• Spiritism	• Tarot Cards
• Buddhism	• Unity	• Gay Church	• Palmistry
• Hinduism	• Science of Mind	• Oriental Mysticism	• Black Magic
• Taoism	• Christian Science	• Rosicrucians	• Satanism
• Muhammadanism	• Metaphysics	• Reincarnation	• Mormonism
• Confucianism	• Voodoo	• Study of Astrology	• Masonic Orders
• T.M.	• Roman Catholic Institution		
They All Sidestep the Fact that Jesus Christ Is God Almighty According to the Authorized Bible.[27]			

Here is a movie recommendation for you, dear reader. A movie titled "Paradise Found" staring Kiefer Sutherland as Paul Gauguin. The movie is the true story of Gauguin's experience with native island people and missionaries in the South Sea Islands. Missionaries are people who go to foreign places to tell people that their God or Gods are no good and the only way to salvation is to convert to the missionaries' religion. I wonder why they call sex with the man on top the missionary position.

The movie "Paradise Found" was shown on STARZ Channel seven times in 2004.

---

[27]Chick Publications, Chino, CA, August 1972, p. 41.

In the movie Christian missionaries are shown burning the wooden statues of the South Sea Islanders God. The goal of the missionaries is to burn every statue so the islanders will convert to Christianity.

Christians pray that "Jesus will be adored by every land and nation. Jesus is the salvation of the world." Christianity and George Bush, a *born-again Christian*, are aiming to convert the whole world.

"My religion consists of a humble admiration of the illimitable superior spirit who reveals himself in the slight details we are able to perceive with our frail and feeble mind."[28]

"Say nothing of my religion. It is known to God and myself alone. Its evidence before the world is to be sought in my life: if it has been honest and dutiful to society the religion which has regulated it cannot be a bad one."[29]

---

[28]Einstein, Albert. (1879-1955).

[29]Jefferson, Thomas. (1743-1826).

CHAPTER IV

Question #2

Do we learn about God by reading the Bible? Do we learn about God's morals and His justice by reading the Bible? Do you believe what the Bible says about God is true?

Do you believe God would send two female bears to maul and tear forty-two children for laughing or calling a man baldhead?

2 Kings 2:24
> He turned around, looked at them and called down a curse on them in the name of the Lord. Then two bears came out of the woods and mauled forty-two of the youths.

Do you believe God would kill a man who would spill his sperm on the ground rather than father a child by his brother's wife?

Genesis 38:10
> What he did was wicked in the Lord's sight; so he put him to death also.

Do you believe God would kill seventy thousand people for taking a census?

2 Samuel 24:10-15

> David was conscience-stricken after he had counted the fighting men, and he said to the Lord, "I have sinned greatly in what I have done. Now, O Lord, I beg you, take away the guilt of your servant. I have done a very foolish thing."
>
> Before David got up the next morning, the word of the Lord had come to Gad the prophet. David's seer: "Go and tell David, 'This is what the Lord says: I am giving you three options. Choose one of them for me to carry out against you.'"
>
> So Gad went to David and said to him, "Shall there come upon you three years of famine in your land? Or three months of fleeing from your enemies while they pursue you? Or three days of plague in your land? Now then, think it over and decide how I should answer the one who sent me."
>
> David said to Gad, "I am in deep distress. Let us fall into the hands of the Lord, for his mercy is great; but do not let me fall into the hands of men."
>
> So the Lord sent a plague on Israel from that morning until the end of the time designated, and seventy thousand of the people from Dan to Bathsheba died.
>
> Do you believe God would kill two hundred fifty men for offering incense to God in worship?

Numbers 16:35

Moses said to Korah, "You and all your followers are to appear before the Lord tomorrow–you and they and Aaron. Each man is to take his censer and put incense in it–250 censers in all–and present it before the Lord. You and Aaron are to present your censers also." So each man took his censer, put fire and incense in it, and stood with Moses and Aaron at the entrance to the Tent of Meeting. When Korah had gathered all his followers in opposition to them at the entrance to the Tent of Meeting, the glory of the Lord appeared to the entire assembly. The Lord said to Moses and Aaron, "Separate yourselves from this assembly so I can put an end to them at once."

But Moses and Aaron fell face down and cried out, "O God, God of the spirits of all mankind, will you be angry with the entire assembly when only one man sins?"

Then the Lord said to Moses, "Say to the assembly, 'Move away from the tents of Korah, Dathan and Abiram.'"

Moses got up and went to Dathan and Abiram, and the elders of Israel followed him. He warned the assembly, "Move back from the tents of these wicked men! Do not touch anything belonging to them or you will be swept away because of all their sins." So they moved away from the tents of Korah, Dathan and Abiram. Dathan and Abiram had come out and were standing with their wives, children and little ones at the entrance to their tents.

Then Moses said, "This is how you will know that the Lord has sent me to do all these things and that it was not my idea. If these men die a natural death and experience only what usually happens to men, then the Lord has not sent me. But if the Lord brings about something totally new, and the earth opens its mouth and swallows them, with everything that belongs to them, and they go down alive into the grave, then you will know that these men have treated the Lord with contempt."

As soon as he finished saying all this, the ground under them split apart and the earth opened its mouth and swallowed them, with their households and all Korah's men and all their possessions. They went down alive into the grave, with everything they owned; the earth closed over them, and they perished and were gone from the community. At their cries, all the Israelites around them fled, shouting. "The earth is going to swallow us too!"

And fire came out from the Lord and consumed the 250 men who were offering the incense.

Do you believe God would send an angel to slaughter 185,000 Assyrian soldiers?

2 Kings 19:35
That night the angel of the Lord went out and put to death a hundred and eighty-five thousand men in the Assyrian camp. When the people got up

the next morning–there were all the dead bodies! So Sennacherib king of Assyria broke camp and withdrew. He returned to Nineveh and stayed there.

Do you believe God would kill 70 men for looking into the ark of the covenant?

I Samuel 6:19
> But God struck down some of the men of Beth Shemesh, putting seventy of them to death because they had looked into the ark of the Lord. The people mourned because of the heavy blow the Lord had dealt them.

Do you believe God would kill 120,000 people forsaking the Lord?

2 Chronicles 28:6
> In one day Pekah son of Remaliah killed a hundred and twenty thousand soldiers in Judah–because Judah had forsaken the Lord, the God of their fathers.

Would your God devour men with fire who complained?

Numbers 11:1
> Now the people complained about their hardships in the hearing of the Lord, and when he heard them his anger was aroused. Then fire from the Lord burned among them and consumed some of the outskirts of the camp.

Would your God kill children as an experiment to test their parents' loyalty like God did to Job? Then God tells Job he passed the test and gave him new children. If God killed your children in an experiment or test, how would you react? Really imagine it, how would you react?

Where in the Bible does God or Jesus smile or laugh in a happy way?

What do you think of the following two quotes?

> I have also been reading the Old Testament, a most bloodthirsty and perilous book for the young. Jehovah is beyond a doubt the worst character in fiction (Robinson, Edwin Arlington, 1969-1933).[30]
>
> [The Bible] has noble poetry in it; and some clever fables; and some blood-drenched history; and some good morals; and a wealth of obscenity; and upwards of a thousand lies (Twain, Mark, 1835-1910, American writer).[31]

Write your answers on the Internet for all the world to see.

---

[30]Robinson, Edwin Arlington. (1869-1933). American poet.

[31]Twain, Mark. (1835-1910), American writer.

CHAPTER V

Question #3

How does this world we live in work?

    Does your religion believe that God interacts with humankind? Does God perform miracles? Does God answer prayers? Does God protect us?
    Do you believe everything that happens is predestined to happen "according to the plan of God who works out everything in conformity with the purpose of His will?" Are plans for people's lives ordained and planned by God before the people are born?
    Does God know the future? Is it part of his plan? Why in Exodus 7:3 does God say, "I will harden Pharaoh's heart and though miraculous signs and wonders He will not listen to you? Then I will lay my hand on Egypt with mighty acts of judgement. I will bring out my people the Israelites." Then in Exodus 9:12 "But the Lord hardened Pharaoh's heart and he would not listen to Moses and Aaron, just as the Lord had said to Moses." Did Pharaoh have a choice or did the Lord tell Moses what the Lord would do to Pharaoh's heart even before Moses went to Pharaoh? Did God want to send the plagues? Did God want to show his power by killing innocent Egyptian babies and animals (all firstborn living in Egypt)? Did

God want Egyptian babies living hundreds of miles from Pharaoh being killed by the angel of death? Why?

Does God protect us? If you were on the phone with your child who lived right next door to you and you were very strong and powerful and your child started screaming for help, what would you do? Would you let a murderer get away to kill your other children? Read the article about the worshiper in church (God's Phone Booth) and give some explanations as to why God did not protect his worshippers? If God did not hear their screaming prayers, why will he hear yours? Will he protect and help you?

> Manila, Philippines—Gunmen on the strife-torn southern Philippine island of Mindanao used assault rifles and machetes Sunday to attack worshipers in a remote Protestant church, killing 39, including women and infants, military reports in Manila said.
>
> Three of the victims were said to have been beheaded, including the lay pastor conducting the service and his brother, said to be the leader of a local anti-communist vigilante movement, military officials said.[32]

Does God answer prayers? Why doesn't he talk to the eighteen young people who today will pray and search and question and then kill themselves, making suicide the third leading cause of death among youngsters in the United States? Did God talk to and help the eighteen young people who committed suicide yesterday, the eighteen who will commit suicide today, the eighteen who will do it tomorrow? Does God answer prayers? Why doesn't he help the forty thousand children who pray and hope and will die today from hunger and disease? If you

---

[32]The Washington Post.

die today it will be forty thousand one, will that make a difference to God? What prayers has God answered for you today?

Do you believe as it says in Isaiah 3:10-11, "Tell the righteous it shall be well with them?" Here is a quote from the book *When Bad Things Happen to Good People*.

> But when they were stunned by tragedy, they reverted back to the basic belief that God punishes people for their sins. They sat there feeling that their daughter's death had been their fault; had they been less selfish and less lazy about the Yom Kippur fast some six months earlier, she might still be alive. They sat there angry at God for having exacted His pound of flesh so strictly, but afraid to admit their anger for fear that He would punish them again. Life had hurt them, and religion could not comfort them. Religion was making them feel worse.
>
> The idea that God gives people what they deserve, that our misdeeds cause our misfortune, is a neat and attractive solution to the problem of evil at several levels, but it has a number of serious limitations. As we have seen, it teaches people to blame themselves. It creates guilt even where there is no basis for guilt. It makes people hate God, even as it makes them hate themselves. And most disturbing of all, it does not even fit the facts.
>
> Perhaps if we had lived before the era of mass communications, we could have believed this thesis, as many intelligent people of those centuries did. It was easier to believe then. You needed to ignore fewer cases of bad things happening to good people. Without newspapers

and television, without history books, you could shrug off the occasional death of a child or of a saintly neighbor. We know too much about the world to do that today. How can anyone who recognizes the names Auschwitz and My Lai, or has walked the corridors of hospitals and nursing homes, dare to answer the question of the world's suffering by quoting Isaiah: "Tell the righteous it shall be well with them?" To believe that today, a person would either have to deny the facts that press upon him from every side, or else redefine what he means by "righteous" in order to fit the inescapable facts. We would have to say that a righteous person was anyone who lived long and well, whether or not he was honest and charitable, and a wicked person was anyone who suffered, even if that person's life was otherwise commendable.[33]

Like every reader of this book, I pick up the daily paper and fresh challenges to the idea of the world's goodness assault my eyes: senseless murders, fatal practical jokes, young people killed in automobile accidents on the way to their wedding or coming home from their high school prom. I add these stories to the personal tragedies I have known, and I have to ask myself: Can I, in good faith, continue to teach people that the world is good, and that a kind and loving God is responsible for what happens in it?

It is tempting at one level to believe that bad things happen to people (especially other people) because God is a righteous judge who gives them exactly what they deserve. By believing that, we

---

[33] *When Bad Things Happen to Good People.*

keep the world orderly and understandable. We give people the best possible reason for being good and for avoiding sin. And by believing that, we can maintain an image of God as all-loving, all-powerful and totally in control.[34]

Why does God interact with Jewish people in the Bible over and over again even in such detail as telling them how to cook and eat and protecting them and helping them and then in the Holocaust God does nothing day after terrible day?
How does this world we live in work? Does God know the future? Is everything already planned by God or do things happen without God's interaction?

Doesn't God say he will harden Pharaoh's heart?

Here is a list taken from the *Complete Book of Bible Trivia*.

1. What strongman was ordained before birth to deliver Israel from the Philistines?
     Samson (Judges 13:2-5)
2. What child, who later ministered with the priest Eli, was ordained before birth to serve God?
     Samuel (1 Samuel 1:11-20)
3. What apostle was foreordained to minister to the Gentiles?
     Paul (Galatians 1:15)
4. What kinsman of Christ was ordained to be his forerunner?
     John the Baptist (Luke 1:13-17)

---

[34]Ibid.

5. What Greek ruler's reign is usually considered to be predicted in the Book of Daniel?
   Alexander the Great (Daniel 11:2-4)
6. What prophet was ordained before birth to be God's messenger?
   Jeremiah (1:5)
7. What king of Judah had his birth and reign foretold to King Jeroboam?
   Josiah (1 Kings 13:2)
8. What psalm, usually assumed to have been written by David, talks about God knowing him before his birth?
   Psalm 139
9. Who foretold Jesus' birth and ministry to Mary?
   The angel Gabriel (Luke 1:26-38)[35]

Did God communicate with the writers of the Bible and tell them what to write?

Does God answer prayers? Does God protect us from bad things that makes us suffer, that cripple us, that kill us?

Why doesn't God perform miracles and answer prayers of people: The prayers of children dying daily of hunger and disease; the prayers of six million Jews in Germany?

What prayers has God answered for you? Be specific.

Here is your space

---

[35] *The Complete Book of Bible Trivia*, pp. 173-174

Does your religion believe that God performs miracles all over the world by changing bread and wine to flesh and blood of Christ (the miracle called transubtantiation)? Does God perform miracles whenever called on by a priest?

A German death camp guard said to Jews after the camp had been operating, murdering Jews for years, day after day after day: "My God is alive and well. Too bad about yours."

Here is a quote from Stierlin Helm, talking about Hitler:
> He was not only responsible–as few in history have been solely responsible–for the planned extermination of millions of Jews and Poles and for the deaths of tens of millions who died in the ensuing war, but also for bringing an abiding disillusionment in the humanity of the human species. When the country of Goethe, Schiller, Mann, Bach, Beethoven and Kant could be swayed to approve if not participate in massive genocide and to close its eyes to the practice of mass sadism, it became apparent that civilized behavior is but a thin veneer for a significant proportion of people. Christianity, the primary ethical force in the western world, suffered a devastating blow when it became apparent that its beliefs, teachings and dictates as well as many of its vicars failed in the very heartland of Christian piety. For many, disbelief in the existence of God became preferable to belief that their God could permit such cruelty and suffering.[36]

---

[36]Stierlin, Helm, p. 10.

Question #3

How does this world we live in work? Is God in control, does he interact with humankind and punish the wicked and protect and reward the good? Does he answer prayers with action and results? Address your answer to the families of the 40,000 children who will die **today** from hunger and disease.

If you believe God is omnipotent and omnipresent, write a message to explain the Tsunami to the families of the 225,000 victims. Was it an act of God? Is God in control or not?

> "This whole act's immutably decreed. 'Twas rehearsed by thee and me a billion years before this ocean rolled. Fool! I am the Fates' lieutenant; I act under orders."[37]

Write your message here:

---

[37] Melville, Herman. "Moby Dick."

CHAPTER VI

Question #4

Do you eat your God?

Many ancient religious ate their gods.

Does your religion teach that you eat your God? Does your religion believe in the miracle transubtantiation? Do you believe that the miracle of the wafer and wine changing to actual flesh and blood occurring thousands of times weekly at the request of priests but on that same day no miracle occurs for the forty-thousand children who die of hunger and disease?

The priest or minister prays before the congregation.

> Almighty God, we pray that your angel may take this sacrifice to your altar in heaven.
> Then, as we receive from this altar the sacred body and blood of your Son, let us be filled with every grace and blessing.
> [Through Christ our Lord. Amen.]
>
> Let your Spirit come upon these gifts to make them holy, so that they may become for us the body and blood of our Lord, Jesus Christ.

Father, may this Holy Spirit sanctify these offerings.
Let them become the body and blood of Jesus Christ our Lord as we celebrate the great mystery which he left us as an everlasting covenant.

May all of us who share in the body and blood of Christ be brought together in unity by the Holy Spirit.

Here is a quote from "Eating the God: The Custom."
Eating the god. The custom of eating the body of a god is known in many communities although the mystery of the Christian sacrament of communion has made it difficult for ethnographers and theologians to see other customs elsewhere with sufficient objectivity to present satisfactory accounts of the profound human impulses involved in consuming the very body and blood of God. Frazer's account is elaborate and his parallels are suggestive. The ceremonial eating of the first-fruits, or the ceremonial eating of bread made from the last sheaf, are connected with the belief that the god (often referred to as the "corn god") resides in the first or the last fruits and must be eaten to assure continued crops, that is, his and our immortality. Frazer connects the ceremonial eating of the cereal itself, even when not baked into a loaf or shaped into human form, with the eating of the god. In Yorkshire a clergyman cut the first corn and made it into communion bread. Peasants in the Volga region ate new cornbread handed them by the priest and prayed. In the Celebes the priest collected the first rice, ground it into meal and gave it to the

villagers. They harvested the rest of the cereal only after all had partaken. Similar customs have been reported from India and Indochina. Among the Ashanti and the Zulu an orgy followed the celebration.

The North American Creek Indians began such a ceremony by cleaning their houses and clothes. They fasted for two nights and one day and purged themselves so that the old food would not mingle in their stomachs with the new food. They built a new fire with the thought that the new fire would burn out their old sins. They then ate ceremonially the grain and, by it, the corn spirit. Twice a year the pre-Columbian Aztecs ceremonially ate bread which, having been consecrated, became the very body of God, and taught that sacramental food was contaminated when it touched other food. The Ainus of northern Japan and Kamchatka eat the bear god (the bear is either considered as god himself or as a divine messenger to the other gods) in a ceremony which is more striking than Frazer's report of the ceremonial eating of the Ainu millet. Here a bear cub is captured once a year and becomes the pet of the village. As it grows older it is caged beside the house of the chief where it is fed delicacies and is made much of. In the spring the god is murdered with expressions of devotion and great feeling. The blood is drunk and the flesh is eaten. The ceremonial eating of the very body and blood of Christ which is essential in the sacrament of the Christian Eucharist, involves theological discussions which lead beyond the scope of this note. In his *First Epistle to the Corinthians*, Paul reminded the congregation of the seriousness of the custom and repeated to them Christ's clear words about it. Tertullian, Cyprian and Augustine held in effect that the bread and blood as symbols were not the signs of an absent reality but were in some sense what they symbolized and possessed the effect of the reality. In the 8th century, John of Damascus held that the Eucharistic body was identical with that born of Mary. A modern view, summarized in the *Catholic Encyclopedia* is "The Body and Blood of God-man are truly, really and substantially present for the nourishment of our souls." Obviously the eating of the very body of the very god involves complex human impulses which are no less impressive among pagans than they are among Christians.[38]

"The true mystery of the world is the visible, not the invisible."[39]
Do you eat your god?

---

[38]Christians, R. D. *Eating the God,* p. 355.

[39]Wilde, Oscar. (1854-1900).

CHAPTER VII

Question #5

If Mary is "ever virgin" then was the ghost a frequent impregnator, for Mary was the mother of Jesus, James, Joseph, Simon, Judas and at least three daughters. If she was married to Joseph, didn't she have intercourse with her own husband?

Matthew 12: 46-47
> While Jesus was still talking to the crowd, his mother and brothers stood outside, wanting to speak to him. Someone told him, "Your mother and brothers are standing outside, wanting to speak to you."

Matthew 13: 55-56
> Isn't this the carpenter's son? Isn't his mother's name Mary and aren't his brothers James, Joseph, Simon, and Judas? Aren't all his sisters with us? Where then did this man get all these things?"

John 7:5
> For even his own brothers did not believe in him.

Mark 3:31

His mother and his brothers arrived. Standing outside they sent word to him and called him.

Luke 8:19
Then his mother and his brothers came to him but were unable to join him because of the crowd.

Matthew 27:56
Among them were Mary Magdalene, and Mary the mother of James and Joseph, and the mother of Zebedee's sons."

If you want to believe Mary is ever virgin you must fabricate some story. Deal with the fact that the Bible says Jesus had brothers and sisters. The Catholic Church has maintained that Joseph was married before he married Mary and the brothers and sisters of Jesus were from Joseph's first wife. If this was true where were Jesus's older brothers and sisters at the nativity scene? Did Joseph and Mary ever consummate their marriage? Didn't Joseph ever make love to his wife? Didn't Mary ever make love to her husband?

Would God make a 14-year-old child pregnant? Here is a quote from the *Book of Lists*.

1. The Virgin Mary
Women customarily married at a very young age in biblical times. The mother of Jesus Christ would not have been an exception. Historians of the period feel she was about 14 when she was espoused to Joseph the Carpenter.[40]

The Bible clearly states that Joseph had relations (sexual intercourse) with Mary after Jesus was born.

---

[40]*The Book of Lists*.

Matthew 1:25
> He had no relations with her until she bore a son, and he named him Jesus.

The Real Family of Jesus – Discovery Channel Store
> Most people know very little about Jesus' family members – who they were, how many there were and what role they played in his life as rebel leader and founder of a new religious movement. For the first time, a team of archaeologists and biblical historians reveal that Jesus was part of a large extended family – a network of relations that played a critical part in his upbringing and in the rise and success of Christianity.
>
> Learn how, in a society that promoted the "extended family," Jesus was well supported and even inspired by his cousin John the Baptist, his grandfather Joachim, his uncle Clophas and more. Evidence from the gospels and recent archaeological finds reveal that Jesus' family was a dynastic clan that believed it was descended from King David. Like all dynasties, it did everything in its power to promote and perpetuate its lineage. But what they would never know is how well they would succeed.

CHAPTER VIII

Question #6

There are more stars than grains of sand on all the beaches in the world. Our sun is one of those stars. Our sun is not even a large sun. Our galaxy is not near the center of the universe. For every person on earth there are a **billion** suns in the universe.

Wasn't the church so mad at Galileo Galilei for saying the earth wasn't at the center of the universe, that our position was not one of importance.

The universe is 10 to 15 billion years old. Put that time on a 24-hour clock and mankind does not appear in the universe until 23 hours and 55 minutes have passed. On this clock it is only 5 minutes from cave man to 2005.

Now the **Question**. Is the Christian view that for billions and billions of years God the Creator and His angels were happy with the universe God created. Then God created man and in the relative time of five minutes man **killed** the Creator's son?

For billions and billions of years was it just God and the Holy Ghost, then in the last 2000 years it became God, the Holy Ghost, and Jesus?

CHAPTER IX

The Supernatural

Question #7

Do you believe in a whole host of Supernatural Beings who are watching you all the time?

Place these supernatural beings in their supernatural hierarchy. #1 being the highest level of supernatural being. Cross out any beings that are not members of your supernatural universe.

God	Apostles	Principalities
Saints	Buddha	Dominations
Jesus	Archangel Gabriel	Powers
The Virgin Mary	Melchizedek	Virtues
The Holy Ghost	Disciples	Spirits
Jehovah	Prince of This World	Ghosts
Yahweh	Demons	Souls
The Holy Spirit	Satan	Vampires
Confucius	Seraphim	Witches
Mohammed	Archangels	The Devil
Allah	Cherubim	Werewolf
Prophets	Thrones	

CHAPTER X

Question #8

Does God do miracles? When nuns and other holy people professed the miracle of the stigmata was a personal God interacting with that person? Was there a divine presence? The people experiencing the stigmata "sent from God" only had knowledge of the crucifixion the way it is always pictured in paintings with nails in the hands. Surely, God knows that Jesus bled from the nail holes in his wrists like thousands of others crucified in Roman times. These people were bleeding from the wrong place. Would these people have bled from their big toe if they thought it would make their story more believable? Do you believe that these people themselves by their own actions caused their own bodies to bleed and falsely called it the work of God or do you believe God made them bleed even in the wrong place?

Hebrew accounts of events in Egypt were not written down until about 50 years later. Is it possible that 50 years later when the Hebrew accounts' of events in Egypt were finally written down that these written accounts were incorrect? Did the story of Moses leading the Hebrews out of Egypt change over those 50 years?

The Egyptians had writings from over fifteen hundred years before the time of Moses. At the time of Moses writing was common throughout Egypt. Everything was written down, even the number of bricks made. Imagine what an event the Nile turning to **blood** and a first born dying in every house was to the Egyptians. Why is there not one mention of these events in the numerous Egyptian records? How can this be?

Babylonian writing started three thousand b.c.e. Nebuchadnezzar lived (605-562 b.c.e.). In Babylonian records is any mention of a handwriting on a wall or men not burning in fire? Babylonians had used writing for over twenty-five hundred years at the time of these events.

What does Assyrian writing say about the battle led by King Sennacherib against Israel and according to the Bible the angel of the Lord went into the Assyrian camp while they were sleeping and put to death eighty-five thousand? Did God do these "miracles" or not?

Is there some other explanation?

CHAPTER XI

Question #9

Were the ideas of immortality of the soul, everlasting life, redemption from transgressions, and magical powers unique to Jesus Christ?

Did the Greeks have all of these very same ideas six hundred years before Jesus Christ?

Could it be that deities were merely earthly rulers whom the gratitude or adulation of their subjects had raised to a place in heaven? Could this be what happened with Jesus Christ?

Is it true that heavenly divine birth stories were told about Alexander the Great and Apolloncus of Tyona? Was it told in the Dead Sea scrolls that Noah's mother was made pregnant by an angel? Can you name one miracle or supernatural event or act involving Jesus Christ that was exclusive to him? Is there any miracle supposedly performed by Jesus that in human history had not been attributed to some other person or God?

When Jesus prayed to his father in heaven and then ascended into heaven and sat at the right hand of God, how many gods are we talking about? Explain as if to a person of the Islamic, Hindu or Buddhist faith.

Is it true that for the Hebrews, Yahweh was the god of Israel and of its fortunes, but the worship of other gods was deemed appropriate at least for Solomon's foreign wives and other politically significant aliens living within Yahweh's territory?

Is it true the Question was not whether other gods existed but a question of which god is sovereign in the land of the Israelites?

Here is a quote from "U.S. News & World Report."
> In some circles, the term "resurrection" itself has become a matter of debate. What does the Bible mean when it says God raised Jesus from the dead? Christian tradition says Jesus was physically resurrected, that his dead flesh and bones were miraculously reanimated. But some theologians have sought to reconcile the resurrection with a more rationalist view by describing it as a metaphor appropriated by early Christians who "thought mythically" and for whom a resurrection of their fallen leader had occurred "in their hearts and minds."[41]

Here is the text of a flyer I found by Lake Pontchartrain about 10 years ago.
> In the name of Allah most gracious - most merciful there is no god but Allah and Muhammad is the last prophet and messenger of Allah. Oh people of the scripture, we invite you to what will make you successful in this world and in the here-after, that is to believe in the oneness of Allah = (God) and all of his prophets that is to believe god has no sons, no daughters, no partners. That is to accept Islam as the way of life for all of humanity. Come to the truth - come to Islam. We invite you

---

[41]Sheler, J. L. "U.S. News & World Report," April 16, 1990.

to come to Mosque Al-HAQQ, Rt 2, Box 517A, Silver Creek, MS 39663. 601 587-0245.

Peace

CHAPTER XII

Question #10

Can we know about Jesus by reading the Bible?
Do you believe that coming back from the dead is one of the main ways we know Jesus was the Son of God? Is it true that on over ten occasions people in the Bible were resurrected from the dead? Is it true that <u>vast numbers</u> of people rose from the dead? Is it true that bones came to life, that holy people came out of their graves and appeared to people in the town? Is it true that at least six other people besides Jesus raised people from the dead? Is it true that just touching Elisha's bones could make a man come back from the dead? Do you believe a witch could bring people back from the dead?

Back from the dead:

Person Doing the Resurrection	**Person Resurrected**
1. Witch of Endor (I Samuel 28)	Samuel
2. Paul (Acts 20:9-10)	Eutychus
3. Jesus (John 11)	Lazarus Man of Bethany
4. Elisha (2 Kings 13)	Bones of Dead Men
5. Jesus' Death (Matthew 27: 52-58)	Holy people out of graves

Person Doing the Resurrection	**Person Resurrected**
6. Jesus (Luke 8:53-55)	Jarius' daughter
7. Jesus (Luke 7:11-12)	Widow's son
8. Elisha (2 Kings 4:32-35)	Son of Shunammite woman
9. Ezekiel (Ezekiel 37:9-10)	A vast army from bones

#1 **Witch** (1 Samuel 28:7, 11, 15)
Then Saul said to his servants, "Find me a woman who is a medium, to whom I can go to seek counsel through her." His servants answered him, "There is a woman in Endor who is a medium, the Witch of Endor." Then the woman asked him, "Whom do you want me to conjure up?" and he answered, "Samuel."
Samuel then said to Saul, "Why do you disturb me by conjuring me up?"
Saul rose from the dead!

#2 **Paul** (Acts 20:9-10)
. . . and a young man named Eutychus who was sitting on the window sill was sinking into a deep sleep as Paul talked on and on. Once overcome by sleep, he fell down from the third story and when he was picked up, he was dead. Paul went down, threw himself upon him, and said as he embraced him, "Don't be alarmed; there is life in him."
Eutychus rose from the dead!

#3 **Jesus** (John 11: 14, 17, 43-44)
Finally Jesus said plainly: "Lazarus is dead."
When Jesus arrived at Bethany, he found that Lazarus had already been in the tomb four days.
Having said this, he called loudly, "Lazarus, come out!" The dead man came out bound head and foot with linen strips, his face wrapped in a cloth. "Untie him," Jesus told them, "and let him go free."

Lazarus rose from the dead!

#4 **Elisha** (2 Kings 13)
Again, for the third time, Ahaziah sent a captain with his company of fifty men. When the third captain arrived, he fell to his knees before Elijah, pleading with him. "Man of God," he implored him, "let my life and the lives of these fifty men, your servants, count for something in your sight!"
Fifty men rose from the dead!

#5 **Jesus' Death** (Matthew 27:52, 53)
The earth quaked, boulders split, tombs opened.
Many bodies of saints who had fallen asleep were raised. After Jesus' resurrection they came forth from their tombs and entered the holy city and appeared to many.
Holy people rose from the dead!

#6 **Jesus** (Luke 8:53-55)
And they ridiculed him, because they knew that she was dead. But he took her by the hand and called to her, "Child arise!" Her breath returned and she immediately arose. He then directed that she should be given something to eat.
Jarius' daughter rose from the dead!

#7 **Jesus** (Luke 7:14, 15)
Then he stepped forward and touched the litter; at this, the bearers halted. He said, "Young man, I bid you get up." The dead man sat up and began to speak. Then Jesus gave him back to his mother.
Widow's son rose from the dead!

#8 **Elisha** (2 Kings 4:32-35)
When Elisha reached the house, he found the boy lying dead. He went in, closed the door on them both, and prayed to the Lord. Then he lay upon the child on the bed, placing his mouth upon the child's mouth, his

eyes upon the eyes, and his hands upon the hands. As Elisha stretched himself over the child, the body became warm. He arose, paced up and down the room, and then once more lay down upon the boy, who now sneezed seven times and opened his eyes.
Son of a Shunammite woman rose from the dead!

#9 **Ezekiel** (Ezekiel 37:9-10)
Then he said to me: Prophesy to the spirit, prophesy, son of man, and say to the spirit: Thus says the Lord God: From the four winds come, O spirit, and breathe into these slain that they may come to life. I prophesied as he told me, and the spirit came into them; they came alive and stood upright, a vast army.
A vast army from the dead!

Do you believe that the people who knew Jesus best for over twenty-five years took offense at him? Do you believe they said, "They knew Jesus not as a prophet but as a 'carpenter's son?'" Do you believe the people of Jesus' hometown tried to kill him? The people who knew Jesus best for over twenty-five years, what did they think of Jesus? In Jesus' own hometown how did the people feel about him as a prophet? Could it be that the people of his hometown took offense at Jesus?

Did the people of Jesus' hometown lack faith in Jesus? Did they say, "These witnesses in Jesus' own hometown, that they knew Jesus not as a prophet but as a 'carpenter's son?'"

Is it true that even Jesus' own brothers "did not believe in him?"

Matt. 13:55-58
Is he not the carpenter's son? Is not his mother named Mary and his brothers James, Joseph, Simon, and Judas? Are not his sisters all with us? Where did this man get all this? And they took

offense at him. But Jesus said to them, "A prophet is not without honor except in his native place and in his own house. And he did not work many mighty deeds there because of their lack of faith.

John 7:5
> For his brothers did not believe in him.

Is it true on one occasion in Nazareth, Jesus' hometown, all the people listening to him speak became an angry mob and tried to kill him by pushing him off a cliff. Did they identify him as <u>Joseph's son</u>?

Luke 4:29
> They rose up, drove him out of the town, and led him to the brow of the hill on which their town had been built, to hurl him down headlong.

Do the four gospels tell conflicting stories of the resurrection? Do they conflict over people present at the tomb, angels present, over guards at the tomb, over tomb visited, over earthquakes or none, over light or dark, over who was told or telling no one, over whether Jesus was there and appeared alive, over whether the guards became like dead men? Is it true that Jesus walked along and talked with his disciples but they did not recognize him? Is it true the disciples who had known Jesus refused to believe those who claimed to see him after he had risen? When the disciples heard Jesus was alive from Mary Magdalene they did not believe it?
When it was reported by two disciples that Jesus had appeared, the rest did not believe it.
Jesus Genealogy (Luke 3:23-28) (Matthew 1:1-17)

What is the point of two of the four gospels giving the Genealogy of Jesus for forty-one generations down to Joseph, the carpenter, unless that is Jesus' blood line. Why not forty-one generations of Mary's ancestors? Why in Luke, Jesus' Genealogy is the blood line carried down from fifty-seven generations to Joseph the carpenter? Luke says, "Jesus was the son, so it was thought of Joseph." These Genealogy generation blood lines became meaningless unless they are Jesus' blood line. Otherwise these men would not be the Genealogy of Jesus at all. They would not be blood relatives of his at all. Interestingly, Luke starts his Genealogy with Adam, son of God, but he does not end it with Jesus, Son of God. Otherwise, it would begin Adam, son of God, and Jesus, Son of God.

Did the people of Jesus' hometown believe he was the Son of God? Did his own brothers believe he was the Son of God? Did his disciples always believe he was the Son of God? Who did believe Jesus was the Son of God and why did they believe it?

In 93 c.e., Flavius Josephus published his work "Antiquities of the Jews." In it he stated that Jesus of Nazareth was the illegitimate son of a Roman soldier. This statement was made in a televison documentary. I have not personally read Josephus' work. Can anyone verify this information? Please make a post on the Internet with your information.

> "God grant me the Serenity
> to accept the things I cannot change
> Courage to change the things I can
> and Wisdom to know the difference."

CHAPTER XIII

Question #11

Do you believe Adolph Hitler found the idea to give the "order to destroy, kill and annihilate all the jews–young and old, women and little children" in his Christian Bible?

Could it be that Hitler and the S.S. thought of themselves as <u>decent</u> <u>men</u>? Good Catholics? Could it be that the founder of the Protestant Church, Martin Luther, hated the Jews? Could it be that men, other Christians, declared saints, hated the Jews?

Match these quotes with their actual authors.

1. St. John Chrysostoma, Patriarch of Constantinople
2. Martin Luther
3. St. Augustine
4. Saint Louis
5. Adolf Hitler

A. "The most miserable of men are Jews."
B. "Their synagogues should be set on fire. Their homes should likewise be broken down and destroyed. Let us drive them out of the country for all time."
C. "The greatest feeling in the world is to have my sword up to the hilt in a Jew."

D. "The Jews are the Christ killers."
E. "The true image of the Hebrew is Judas Iscariot, who sells the Lord for silver. The Jew can never spiritually understand the scriptures and forever will bear the guilt for the death of Jesus because their fathers killed the savior."
F. "It is incumbent upon all Christians to hate the Jews."
G. His antisemitic tracts that equate Jews with devil worship.

Answers
1. Saint John Chrysostoma said "D" and "F."
2. Martin Luther said "B" and "G."
3. Saint Augustine said "E."
4. Saint Louis said "C."
5. Adolf Hitler said none.

> The murder of six million Jews by baptized Christians, from whom membership in good standing was not (and has not yet been) withdrawn, raises the most insistent question about the credibility of Christianity."[42]

Do you think Hitler read these passages from the Bible?
Esther 3:6
> Yet having learned who Mordecai's people were, he scorned the idea of killing only Mordecai. Instead Haman looked for a way to destroy all Mordecai's people, the Jews, throughout the whole kingdom of Xerxes.

---

[42]Harper & Row, Publishers, ISBN 0-06-065251-9.

Esther 3:13
> Dispatches were sent by couriers to all the king's provinces with the order to destroy, kill and annihilate all the Jews--young and old, women and little children—on a single day, the thirteenth day of the twelfth month of Adar, and to plunder their goods.

> Such evil deeds could religion prompt.
> <u>Lucretius</u> (96 b.c.e. - 55 b.c.e.) *De Rerum Natura*[43]

> With or without religion, you would have good people doing good things and evil people doing evil things. But for good people to do evil things, that takes religion.
> <u>Steven Weinberg</u> (1933 -), quoted in *The New York Times*, April 20, 1999.[44]

---

[43]<u>Lucretius</u> (96 b.c.e. - 55 b.c.e.), *De Rerum Natura*

[44]Weinberg, S. (1993-), *The New York Times*, April 20, 1999.

CHAPTER XIV

Question #12

Was the Easter celebration of the dead and risen Christ grafted upon a earlier, similar celebration of the dead and risen Adonis? Did the church often skillfully continue to plant the seeds of new faith on the old stock of paganism? Is Easter named after Eastre, the pagan goddess of Spring? The rabbit was Eastre's companion and a symbol of fertility and new life, so we have the Easter bunny today, a pagan symbol.

Did the church pick December 25th as the birthday of Christ because the pagan festival of the winter solstice was on that date? Did the church ignore the evidence that suggests that Christ was born in February? Did the birthday of the Savior replace the birthday of the sun?

Where did the cross worn by the Pope originate? Did the cross as a symbol of worship originate with Christians or pagans? Did Christians and Puritans mutilate crosses because they were pagan symbols?

Does Greek Myth say a god came to earth and impregnated Leda, the wife of King Tyndareus? Were the children of the human female and a god immortal and had everlasting life? Were several mortals believed to be descendants of the god Zeus?

Is it true in Greek mythology long before Jesus Christ that Persephone, the daughter of Demeter, goes to the dark land of the dead, the kingdom of the dead, but after months she comes out into the upper air alive at Springtime (Easter) (The Resurrection) when earth rejoices. The wheat springs up, bright, fresh, and green in the plowland. Flowers unfold, birds sing, and young animals are born. Everywhere the heavens smile for joy or weep sudden showers of gladness upon the springing earth because "Persephone is Risen." Persephone is resurrected from the dead. Was the idea of resurrection being celebrated at spring time used by the Christians to convince or convert believers to believe Jesus could do just what Persephone could do "resurrect from the dead" and cause the earth to rejoice? Did Jesus and Persephone return from the dead to their glad mothers?

The Greek cross, formed of four equal arms at right angles to one another, is thought by some to have had its origin in the two crossed sticks used in the production of fire. Indeed, there is no doubt that this cross was at first a Fire-symbol, and afterwards a Solar emblem; it is the commonest form of cross used by pre-Christian people, and one of its oldest known examples belongs to the Kassite period (1746 b.c.e. to 1171 b.c.e.).

All doubts regarding the sacred character of the pre-Christian Greek cross are dissipated by the description which Sir Arthur Evans gives of an equi-armed cross of white marble standing as the center-piece on an altar of the Queen's private chapel at Knossos: a cross, be it noted, dated by Sir Arthur as previous to 1400 b.c.e.

It is very frequently called the Assyrian cross, and it is found connected with at least three Assyrian kings:

(1) In the British Museum there are representations of Tiglath-Pileser III (745-727 b.c.e.), whose

reign may be regarded as one of the most brilliant in Assyrian history. In one instance at least, he is shown wearing the Assyrian (or Maltese) cross. This was a Sun-symbol, and the king wore it because he was the son of the sun.
(2) It is found worn round the neck of Samsi-Vul IV, King of Assyria, *circa* 835 b.c.e.
(3) It is also to be seen with other symbols on a stele of Samsi-Adad VI, *circa* 824 b.c.e.
The crosses found connected with these Assyrian kings are paralleled by the cross found in the grave of St. Cuthbert, and by the cross worn by the Pope today.[45]

"Religion is the opium of the masses" (Karl Marx).[46]

According to Marx, religion is an expression of material realities and economic injustice. Thus, problems in religion are ultimately problems in society. Religion is not the disease, but merely a symptom. It is used by oppressors to make people feel better about the distress they experience due to being poor and exploited. This is the origin of his comment that religion is the "opium of the masses."[47]

---

[45]*Cornish Crosses: Christian and Pagan,* pp. 25; 28.

[46]Marx, Karl

[47]Retrieved from http://atheism.about.com/od/philosophyofreligion/a/marx.htm

CHAPTER XV

Question 13

To believe in God or in a guiding force because someone tells you to is the height of stupidity. We are given senses to receive our information within. With our own eyes we see, and with our own skin we feel. With our intelligence, it is intended that we understand. But each person must puzzle it out for himself or herself. (Sophy Burnham)[48]

The more I study religions the more I am convinced that man never worshiped anything but himself. (Sir Richard Francis Burton)[49]

A myth is a religion in which no one any longer believes. (James Feibleman)[50]

Once upon a time a group of people lived in a far off land and they had several strange ideas. They believed

---

[48]Burnham, S.

[49]Burton, Sr Richard. (1821-1890).

[50]Feibleman, James.

that their god Zeus came to earth and took a beautiful maiden for his bride. They believed Zeus and his bride Danae had a son Perseus.

Now Perseus was a real person and so was his mother Danae. The people believed that Perseus was a god and had supernatural powers and would live forever up high on Mt. Olympus. They also believed they could live again with Perseus in the Kingdom of the Olympians.

They believed that only the followers of Perseus would be alive again up high on Mt. Olympus. These people believed that only members of their group would go to happy Mt. Olympus when they die. They believed other non-believers would go to some other place and be tortured.

If you moved to this land would you believe the story about Perseus and become one of his followers so you could go to Mt. Olympus when you died?

Answer "yes" or "no."
And explain why!

Here is your space

Here is a quote from *Gods, Men and Monsters from the Greek Myths* by Michael Gibson.

> The thunder-god spied the lonesome maiden through the opening in the roof, and in the shape of a golden shower he descended to her. No longer was Danae lonesome, for now she was the happy bride of Zeus. But when her father heard the cries of an infant from her chamber he broke through the walls in a rage, intending to kill his grandson. When he learned that Zeus was the child's father he did not dare to lay hands on him. Instead he put Danae and her son, Perseus, in a chest and threw it into the sea.[51]

---

[51]Gibson, Michael, *Gods, Men and Monsters from the Greek Myths*. Schocken Books.

Now, I will change the names, substitute the new names and you should reanswer Question #13.

Zeus	=	Jehovah
Danae	=	Mary
Perseus	=	Jesus
Mt. Olympus	=	Heaven
Olympians	=	Angels

Once upon a time a group of people lived in a far off land and they had several strange ideas. They believed that their god Jehovah came to earth and took a beautiful maiden for his bride. They believed Jehovah and his bride Mary had a son Jesus.

Now Jesus was a real person and so was his mother Mary. The people believed that Jesus was a god and had supernatural powers and would live forever up high in Heaven. They also believed they could live again with Jesus in the Kingdom of the Angels.

They believed that only the followers of Jesus would be alive again up high in Heaven. These people believed that only members of their group would go to happy Heaven when they die. They believed other non-believers would go to some other place and be tortured.

If you moved to this land would you believe the story about Jesus and become one of his followers so you could go to Heaven when you died?

Now will you become a follower so you can go to heaven when you die?

Answer "yes" or "no" and explain why.

Here is your space

Following is the sad account of the life of a once prominent and successful evangelist, his slide into unbelief and his rejection of Christianity. In 1996, the book *Farewell to God* was published for all the world to see the author, Charles Templeton, claim:

"I oppose the Christian Church because, for all the good it sometimes does, it presumes to speak in the name of God and to propound and advocate beliefs that are outdated, demonstrably untrue, and often, in their various manifestations, deleterious to individuals and to society.

"Why does God's grand design require creatures with teeth designed to crush spines or rend flesh, claws fashioned to seize and tear, venom to paralyze, mouths to suck blood, coils to constrict and smother – even expandable jaws so that prey may be swallowed whole and alive? . . . Nature is in Tennyson's vivid phrase, 'red in tooth and claw,' and life is a carnival of blood.

"How could a loving and omnipotent God create such horrors as we have been contemplating?

"I believe that there is no supreme being with human attributes – no God in the biblical sense – but that all life is the result of timeless evolutionary forces . . . over millions of years.

"I believe that, in common with all living creatures, we die and cease to exist as an entity."

Mithraism

The name Mithras was the Persian word for "contract." Mithras was also known throughout Europe and Asia by the names Mithra, Mitra, Meitros, Mihr, Mehr, and Meher. The veneration of this God began about 4000 years ago in Persia, where it was soon imbedded with Babylonian doctrines.

As a deity connection with the sun and its life-giving powers, Mithras was known as "The Lord of the Wide Pastures" who was believed to cause the plants to spring forth from the ground. In the time of Cyrus and Darius the Great, the rulers of Persia received the first fruits of the fall harvest at the festival of Mehragan. At this time they wore their most brilliant clothing and drank wine. In the Persian calendar, the seventh month and the sixteenth day of each month were also dedicated to Methras.

According to Persian mythology, Mithras was born of a virgin given the title "Mother of God." The God remained celibate throughout his life, and valued self-control, renunciation and resistance to sensuality among his worshippers. Mithras represented a system of ethics in which brotherhood was encouraged in order to unify against the forces of evil.

The Persians called Mithras "The Mediator" since he was believed to stand between the light of Ahura-Mazda and the darkness of Ahriman. He was said to have 1000 eyes, expressing the conviction that no man could conceal his wrongdoing from the god. Mithras was known as the God of Truth, and Lord of Heavenly Light, and said to have stated "I am a star which goes with thee and shines out of the depths."

The faithful referred to Mithras as "the Light of the World," symbol of truth, justice, and loyalty. He was mediator between heaven and earth and was a member of a Holy Trinity.

The worshippers of Mithras held strong beliefs in a celestial heaven and an infernal hell. They believed that the benevolent powers of the god would sympathize with their suffering and grant them the final justice of immortality and eternal salvation in the world to come. They looked forward to a final day of judgement in which the dead would resurrect, and to a final conflict that would destroy the existing order of all things to bring about the triumph of light over darkness.

Purification through a ritualistic baptism was required of the faithful, who also took part in a ceremony in which they drank wine and ate bread to symbolize the body and blood of the god. Sundays were held sacred, and the birth of the god was celebrated annually on December the 25th. After the earthly mission of this god had been accomplished, he took part in a Last Supper with his companions before ascending to heaven, to forever protect the faithful from above.

However, it would be a vast oversimplification to suggest that Mithraism was the single forerunner of early Christianity. Aside from Christ and Mithras, there were plenty of other deities (such as Osiris, Tammuz, Adonis, Balder, Attis, and Dionysus) said to have died and resurrected. Many classical heroic figures, such as Hercules, Perseus, and Theseus, were said to have been born through the union of a virgin mother and divine father. Virtually every pagan religious practice and festivity that couldn't be suppressed or driven underground was eventually incorporated into the rites of Christianity as it spread across Europe and throughout the world.[52]

The birthday of the sun became the birthday of the son.

Mithra was miraculously born on December 25.
Shepherds and Magi witnessed Mithra's birth.
Mithra is a savior.
Mithra is a mediator between humans and a higher god.
Mithra is a judge who rewards the eternal souls of good people with eternal salvation, of evil people with eternal damnation.
Mithra died, descended into the earth and was resurrected.
Mithra was called the "Good Shepherd" and pictured carrying a lamb on his shoulders.
Mithra's blood is called the "blood of the Lamb."
Mithra's followers practice a sacred meal of bread and wine.

---

[52]Retrieved December 30, 2004, from http://www.crystalinks.com/mithra.html

Mithra's followers observe Sunday as a holy day.[53]

As Christianity gathered momentum and eventually became the Roman Empire's state religion, Mithraism was not tolerated. The Apologist saw it as a satanic travesty of the holiest rites of their religion. Nevertheless Catholicism has preserved some of the outer forms of Mithraism (to name some: the timing of Christmas, Bishops adaptation of miters as sign of their office, Christian priests becoming "Father" despite Jesus' specific proscription of the acceptance of such title). The Mithraic Holy Father wore a red cap and garment and a ring, and carried a shepherd's staff. The Head Christian adopted the same title and outfitted himself in the same manner.[54]

"The Vatican is a dagger in the heart of Italy."
"The whole religious complexion of the modern world is due to the absence from Jerusalem of a lunatic asylum" (Paine, Thomas).

---

[53]Retrieved December 30, 2004, from http://www.tojustin.com/conclus.htm

[54]Retrieved December 30, 2004, from http://www.crystalinks.com/mithra.html

CHAPTER XVI

Question #14

Are you normal? If more than 50% of a species has a behavioral trait, is that behavior normal for that species? If over 50% of bears hibernate, then hibernation is normal behavior for bears.

If more than 50% of people live as adult couples, then living as couples is normal behavior for the species.

If more than 50% of marriages end in divorce and 55% of married women and 60% of married men are not monogamous but have other sexual partners, then is being monogamous normal behavior for the species?

What is the nature of the beast--is it lifetime monogamy with one sexual partner or a life with more than one sexual partner? Is it normal to have only one sexual partner for your whole life? Is sexually monogamous fidelity the nature of the beast or is it just the opposite?

If over 50% of the houses built in the U.S. collapsed on their occupants and 55% to 60% of the remaining houses leaned some a little, some a lot, what would we do?

Would we get a new set of plans or use a new foundation? Maybe strict monogamy is not the morality of the Bible.

Where does the Bible prohibit polygamy?

The answer according to *The Complete Book of Bible Trivia* by J. S. Lang is that the Bible does not prohibit polygamy.

The first reported polygamist was Lamech (Genesis 4:19).

Gideon had seventy sons by his many wives (Judges 8:30).

Samuel's father had two wives named Hannah and Peninnah (I Samuel 1: 1-2).

Esau had wives named Judith, Bashemath and Mahalath (Genesis 26:24; 28:9).

Saul's wives were named Ahinoam and Rizpha (I Samuel 14:50; 2 Samuel 3:7).

Ahasuerus had wives named Vashti and Ester (Esther 1:10-12; 2:1-17).

David's wives included Abrigail, Maocah, Haggith, and Ezlah (2 Samuel 12:8).

Abraham took Keturah as his third wife (Genesis 16:3; 23:19; 25:1).

Moses had two wives, one of them named Zipporah (Exodus 18:2; Numbers 12:1).

Ahab, influenced by his dominating wife, also had other wives (I Kings 20:7).

God spoke with several of these men on several occasions and not once did he say to them that having more than one wife was a sin. God appears to encourage polygamy by telling Hagar to go back to Abraham and be his second wife instead of staying away and leaving Abraham with only one wife.

Genesis 16:7-15

> The Lord's messenger found her by a spring in the wilderness, the spring on the road to Shur, and he asked, "Hagar, maid of Sarai, where have you come from and where are you going? She

answered, "I am running away from my mistress, Sarai." But the Lord's messenger told her: "Go back to your mistress and submit to her abusive treatment. I will make your descendants so numerous, added the Lord's messenger, that they will be too many to count." Besides, the Lord's messenger said to her:

"You are now pregnant and shall bear a son; you shall name him Ishmael, for the Lord has heard you, God has answered you. He shall be a wild ass of a man, his hand against everyone, and everyone's hand against him; in opposition to all his kin shall he encamp."

To the Lord who spoke to her she gave a name, saying "You are the God of Vision"; she meant, "Have I really seen God and remained alive after my vision?" That is why the well is called Beer-lahai-roi. It is between Kadesh and Bered.

Hagar bore Abram a son, and Abram named the son whom Hagar bore him Ishmael.

God talked to David and listed all the blessings David had received from him.

1. God made you king over Israel.
2. God delivered you from the hands of Saul.
3. God gave your master's house and wives to you.

Then God said that if this had been too little, God could mention more blessings.

II Samuel 12:7-8

Then Nathan said to David: "You are the man! Thus says the Lord God of Israel: 'I anointed you king of Israel. I rescued you from the hand of Saul. I gave you your lord's house and your lord's wives for your own. I gave you the house of Israel and of Judah. And if this were not enough, I could count up for you still more.

When God spoke to David he never mentioned any of David's six-plus wives. But God did find David committed a great sin by taking another man's wife, Bathsheba. The sin was taking another man's wife but having six wives was part of the good things God gave to David. How can God list wives as good things he gave to David if having more than one wife is a sin according to modern religion? God's morals couldn't change in a brief three thousand years. Could they? When man's laws and rules conflict with God's rules, whose should be obeyed?

Why are there so many passages in the Bible where God interacts with people, giving them more than one wife as part of God's plan? According to God's own words in the Bible is it moral for a man to have more than one wife? In the Bible, according to God, is it moral for a man with one wife to take a second woman to be his wife if that second woman is not married already?

Wives of biblical Kings and Leaders

1. Solomon = 700 wives, 300 concubines
2. Reholoam = 18 wives, 60 concubines
3. Odijah = 14 wives
4. David = 6-plus wives, more than 10 concubines
5. Jacob = 2 wives, 2 concubines
6. Josiah = 2 or more wives
7. Elkanah = 2 wives
8. King Joash = 2 or more wives
9. Abraham = 1 wife, several concubines, Sarai and Hagar

CHAPTER XVII

Did You Know???

1. The Garden of Eden was in Iraq.
2. Mesopotamia, which is now Iraq, was the cradle of civilization!
3. Noah built the ark in Iraq.
4. The Tower of Babel was in Iraq.
5. Abraham was from Ur, which is in Southern Iraq!
6. Isaac's wife, Rebekah, is from Nahor which is in Iraq.
7. Jacob met Rachel in Iraq.
8. Jonah preached in Nineveh–which is in Iraq.
9. Assyria, which was in Iraq, conquered the ten tribes of Israel.
10. Amos cried out in Iraq.
11. Babylon, which is in Iraq, destroyed Jerusalem.
12. Daniel was in the lion's den in Iraq!
13. The 3 Hebrew children were in the fire in Iraq.
14. Belshazzar, the King of Babylon, saw the "writing on the wall" in Iraq.
15. Nebuchadnezzar, King of Babylon, carried the captive Jews into Iraq.
16. Ezekiel preached in Iraq.
17. The wise men were from Iraq.
18. Peter preached in Iraq.

19. The "Empire of Man" described in Revelation is called Babylon, which was a city in Iraq.

Israel is the nation most often mentioned in the Bible, but do you know which nation is second? It is Iraq. However, that is not the name that is used in the Bible. The names used in the Bible are Babylon, Land of Shinar, and Mesopotamia. The word Mesopotamia means between two rivers, because it is between the Tigris and Euphrates Rivers.

The name Iraq means country with deep roots. Indeed Iraq is a country with deep roots and is very significant in the Bible; e.g.,

*Eden was in Iraq–Genesis 2:10-14

*Adam & Eve were created in Iraq–Genesis 2:7-8

*Satan made his first recorded appearance in Iraq–Genesis 3:1-6

*Nimrod established Babylon and the Tower of Babel was built in Iraq–Genesis 10:8-98 & 11:1-4

*The confusion of the languages took place in Iraq–Genesis 11:5-11

*Abraham came from a city in Iraq–Uhr of the Chaldees (now Baghdad)–Genesis 11:31 & Acts 7:2-4

*Isaac's bride came from Iraq–Genesis 24:3-4 & 10

*Jacob spent 20 years in Iraq–Genesis 27:42-45 & 31:38

*The first world Empire was in Iraq–Daniel 1:1-2 & 2:36-38

*The greatest revival in history was in a city in Iraq–Jonah 3

*The events of the book of Esther took place in Iraq–Esther

*The book of Nahum was a prophecy against a city in Iraq–Nahum

*The book or Revelation has prophecies against Babylon, which was the old name for the nation of Iraq–Revelation 17 & 18

No other nation, except Israel, has more history and prophecy associated with it than Iraq.

Since America is typically represented by an eagle, Saddam and Bin Laden should have read up on their Muslim passages.

The following verse is from the Holy Quran, Quran (9:11)–For it is written that a son of Arabia would awaken a fearsome Eagle. The wrath of the Eagle would be felt throughout the lands of Allah and lo, while some of the people trembled in despair still more rejoiced; for the wrath of the Eagle cleansed the lands of Allah; and there was peace.

NOT TRUE

10-31-05

Rene J Dartt III

CHAPTER XVIII

Religion is a part of every culture and society. From cave man to modern man, all believe in some mystical, supernatural power greater than themselves. All cultures have a power to pray to, a power to worship in song and dance and ceremony. Men have always offered praise and offerings of sacrifice. All cultures have ceremonies as part of their religious and spiritual lives. All cultures offer their members opportunities and obligations to be one of the group of believers, one of the faithful. Religion, believing and faith are part of the essence of humanity.

But exactly what do you believe and why do you believe it?

What religion are you and why?

Nine-five (95%) percent of people practice and believe the religion they are born into. Whatever religion their mother follows is the same one that they follow. Could it be that we believe what we so strongly hold as the true religion due only to the randomness of our birth location?

We believe what our parents and especially our mothers tell us to believe. If we are born in Iraq, we believe in Islam and the Holy Quran. If we are born in India, we believe in Hinduism. If we are born in Israel, we believe in Judaism and the Torah. If we are born in Thailand, we believe in Buddhism. If we are born in the United States, we believe in Christianity and the Bible.

I bet you, dear reader, that you are the same religion as your mother no matter what that religion may be.

If you are Christian, maybe you believe like the bumper sticker says, "The Bible Says It and I Believe It."

"Real Men Love Jesus."

So here is a challenge to you. Write down what you personally believe. Don't say I am a Catholic and I believe what the church says and teaches. I want you to be specific. What do **you** really believe?

"It is necessary to the happiness of man that he be mentally faithful to himself. Infidelity does not consist in believing, or in disbelieving, it consists in professing to believe what he does not believe" (Paine, Thomas).

A word of caution to you dear reader, be careful because if your true beliefs do not match the dogma of your religion you may be in metaphysical distress. Professing one belief publically and believing something else in your heart and soul will lead to metaphysical distress.

Do you dare to question yourself. Can you write down some of your main beliefs? I would not challenge you to do this without telling you what I believe.

On the last page of this book and on the web site, WWW.DEEPTRUTH.INFO you can read what I personally believe.

My religion is love.

Love is my religion–I could die for it. (John Keats)[55]

---

[55]Keats, John.

Love is patient
Love is kind
It does not envy
It does not boast
It is not proud
It is not rude
It is not self-seeking
It is not easily angered
Keeps no record of wrong
Love does not delight in evil
But rejoices with truth
It always protects, always trusts,
Always hopes, always perseveres.

Now here is your space for your beliefs.

Beliefs

CHAPTER XIX

The Maltese Cross

The Story of the Maltese Cross

When a courageous band of crusaders, the Knights of St. John, fought the Saracens for possession of the Holy Lands, they were faced with a new device of war–fire.

As the crusaders advanced on Jerusalem, the Saracens pelted them with glass bombs full of naphtha and then threw down flaming torches. Hundreds of knights were burned alive while others risked their lives to save their kinsmen from painful fiery deaths. Thus these became the first firefighters. Their heroic efforts were recognized by fellow crusaders who awarded them with a badge of honor similar to the cross firefighters wear today. Since the Knights of St. John lived nearly four centuries on the island of Malta, in the Mediterranean Sea, the cross came to be known as the Maltese Cross.

The Meaning of the Maltese Cross

The Maltese Cross is our symbol of protection. It means that the Firefighter who wears this cross is willing to lay down his/her life for you just as the crusaders sacrificed their lives for their fellow man so many years ago. The Maltese Cross is a Firefighter's badge of honor, signifying that he/she works in courage - a ladder's rung away from death.

A Maltese Cross consists of eight points. The meaning of each point is: courage, perseverance, loyalty, tact, sympathy, dexterity, observation, and explicitness.[56]

---

[56] Retrieved January 2, 2005, from http://www.bfdlocal920.com/kid_maltese.htm

Annotated Bibliography

Knowledge is plentiful; wisdom rare. We encounter wisdom through a trinity of experience. Primarily we become wise through the continual process of self-revelation. Next teachers, or more rightly sages and prophets, point the way to the gift. Finally, . . . from the pages of books.

The following list of twelve texts will give the aspirant the foundation of the world's great ideas and concepts. From these waters the deserts of uncertainty and despair become fertile plains and valleys.

Aristotle (384-322 b.c.e.) collected works. A towering genius. The translator, edition, etc. we leave to the pleasure of the reader.

Bible (2000 b.c.e.-350 c.e.) Old and New Testaments with Apocrypha. The King James Version is recommended as the basic text because of its instrumentality in the formation of modern English. The Bible expresses its ideas, concepts and theology, using approximately 9,000 different words (excluding articles, prepositions, pronouns, etc.).

Bhagavad Gita (Circa 500 b.c.e.) embodiment of Hindu Religious experience. A philosophical and theological masterpiece addressing ontological, epistemological, cosmological and phenomenological concerns.

Confucius (551-479 b.c.e.) Analects of Confucius. One of the three great Chinese literary works (I-Ching and Lao-Tzu are the others). This work formed the basis of Chinese law, ethics, education, politics, etiquette, etc., etc. . . .

Homer (Circa 7th c. b.c.e.) Illiad and Odyssey. "The" Epic poems of Western Civilization.

I-Ching (1150 b.c.e.) a book of philosophy which addresses chance, chaos, change and uncertainty. The preferred translation is John Blofeld's.

Lao-Tzu (c. 575-c. 485 b.c.e.) Tao Te Chi or Lao Tzu. Profound wisdom contained in a small, elegant package.

Plato (c. 429-347 b.c.e.) collected works. Lord Whitehead once remarked that Plato created Western philosophy, and everything subsequent is commentary.

Shakespeare (1564-1616) complete works. The Bard uses almost 15,000 words to express his thoughts (compare to the Bible). He also coined several hundred words, an equal number of aphorisms, epigrams and phrases and expressed a universality about the human condition which is transcendent.

Tibetan Book of the Dead (c. b.c.e.) a journey into a world that awaits us all. Should be read in conjunction with the I-Ching. Remarkable! W. Y. Evans-Wentz translation.

Upanishads (18th century b.c.e.) "to sit at the foot of the Master." Its principal concern is an investigation into the nature of the Atman (Individual self or soul) and its identity with Brahman (universal self or world soul).

Vedas (c. 1500-800 b.c.e.) the concerns of Heisenberg and Hawkin penned three and one-half thousand years ago[57]

---

[57]Klein, Victor C. (1998). *My Motto Is* . . . Metairie, LA: Lycanthrope Press.

BELIEVING

I.   I believe in a power greater than man
II.   I believe in the power of creation
III.   I believe in the power of the Cosmos
IV.   I believe I have a soul, an essence, a being, a life force, a Cosmic force that does not die when my physical body dies
V.   I believe in prayer, soul searching introspective and extrospective thoughts, meditation, oneness with the Cosmos, unity with the Divine Absolute.
VI.   I believe in love and caring, and sharing
VII.   I believe in God as a concept defined by all of these beliefs
VIII.   I believe God is inside me and inside all people
IX.   I believe God is in all religions
X.   God is Love–for mortal to aid mortal–this is God, and this is the road to eternal life.

Book Ordering Information

Copies of *"All Iraqis Are Going to Hell! George W. Bush" and "The Christian Right"* can be ordered

1. By phone toll free dial: 1-800-860-1100, plus Code 718427
2. By mail:
    Reno Jean Daret, III
    6805 Glendale Street
    Metairie, LA 70003
3. On Internet at WWW.DEEPTRUTH.INFO
4. You can find this book on Ebay.
    Just type in:
    All Iraqis Are Going to Hell

Mail orders to:

    Daret Enterprises

    6805 Glendale Street

    Metairie, LA 70003

    Phone: 1-504-417-2979

Cost of book: $10.00 each

    Price includes: tax, handling and postage with tracking in the United States.

Orders will normally be mailed the next business day.

    Pay by personal check or money order, or by using PAYPAL

    Books are available at wholesale prices to businesses, schools, groups, or individuals. You can be a distributor. Call for details.

LOUISIANA AIR NATIONAL GUARD
1977 - 1998

MY CROSS

ORLEANS PARISH
Inner City 6th Grade
1970-1979
JEFFERSON PARISH
Special Education Middle School
Behavior Disordered and
Emotionally Disturbed Students
1991-1999

Teacher's Prayer

I want to teach my students how~To live this life on earth~To face its struggles and its strife and to improve their worth~Not just the lesson in a book~Or how the rivers flow~But how to choose the proper path~Wherever they may go~To understand eternal truth~And know the right from wrong~And gather all the beauty of~A flower and a song~For if I help the world to grow~In wisdom and in grace~Then I shall feel that I have won~And I have filled my place~And so I ask your guidance, God~That I may do my part~For character and confidence~And happiness of heart,

~James J. Metcalfe

MY CROSS